Squanto

1585?–1622

by Arlene B. Hirschfelder

Blue Earth Books

an imprint of Capstone Press
Mankato, Minnesota

Blue Earth Books are published by Capstone Press
151 Good Counsel Drive, P.O. Box 669, Mankato, Minnesota 56002
http://www.capstonepress.com

Library of Congress Cataloging-in-Publication Data
Hirschfelder, Arlene B.
    Squanto, 1585?–1622 / by Arlene B. Hirschfelder.
    p. cm.—(American Indian biographies)
    Summary: A biography of Squanto, a Patuxet Indian who served as translator to the Pilgrims of Plymouth
in what is now Massachusetts and aided them in establishing a successful colony in the early 1600s.
    Includes bibliographical references and index.
    ISBN 0-7368-2446-4 (hardcover)
    1. Squanto—Juvenile literature. 2. Wampanoag Indians—Biography—Juvenile literature. 3. Pilgrims
(New Plymouth Colony)—Juvenile literature. [1. Squanto. 2. Wampanoag Indians—Biography. 3. Indians
of North America—Massachusetts—Biography. 4. Pilgrims (New Plymouth Colony) 5. Plymouth
(Mass.)—History—17th century. 6. Massachusetts—History—Colonial period, ca. 1600-1775.]
I. Title. II. Series.
E99.W2S625 2004
974.4004'97348'0092—dc22   2003013017

Editorial Credits

Editor: Christine Peterson
Series Designers: Jennifer Bergstrom and
    Heather Kindseth
Book Designer: Jennifer Bergstrom
Photo Researcher: Wanda Winch
Product Planning Editor: Eric Kudalis

Photo Credits

Cover images: Carol and Mark Archambault,
alewife fish; Photodisc/Siede Preis, corn kernels;
The Granger Collection, New York, Squanto

American Museum of Natural History Library, 9;
Capstone Press/Gary Sundermeyer, 11, 15;
Haffenreffer Museum of Anthropology, Brown
University, 14, 19; North Wind Picture Archives,
17, 23, 26, 29 (all); Stock Montage Inc., 7, 16;
Tara Prindle, 8, 12; The Granger Collection, New
York, 4, 5, 20–21, 22, 25

1 2 3 4 5 6 09 08 07 06 05 04

Contents

CHAPTER 1

Coming Together

Settlers at Plymouth Colony were surprised to see an Indian walk into their village. Samoset greeted them in English. He later brought Squanto to Plymouth Colony. ➤

On a March day in 1621, Squanto, a Patuxet Wampanoag native, prepared for a journey that would lead him through the wooded areas of what is today New England. His journey would take him to a small village of English settlers called Plymouth Colony.

Squanto, who was also called Tisquantum, dressed in his leather pants and **breechclout**. He slipped into his moccasins. His clothing would protect him from the scratchy plants along the paths in the thick woods.

That day, Squanto would meet Samoset, an Abenaki native from what is today Maine. Squanto and Samoset would be joined by Massasoit, a Wampanoag *sachem,* or leader, and 60 of his people. Together, the men would make the journey to Plymouth.

Squanto was asked to join Massasoit at Plymouth Colony to help the leader speak with the English settlers. Squanto could speak better English than Samoset. Squanto had learned the language years before in England. Translating for the settlers would put Squanto's English skills to the test.

Later that day, the group arrived at Plymouth Colony. Squanto, Samoset, and three of Massasoit's men entered the small village. Massasoit and the rest of his people waited on top of a nearby hill. The Englishmen walked toward the Indians.

▲ *Squanto was a translator and guide for settlers at Plymouth Colony. This 1873 painting is one artist's idea of how Squanto looked. Squanto did not have a portrait done during his lifetime.*

Squanto saw that the men were carrying guns. Squanto quickly explained that the Indians wanted to have peace talks with the settlers.

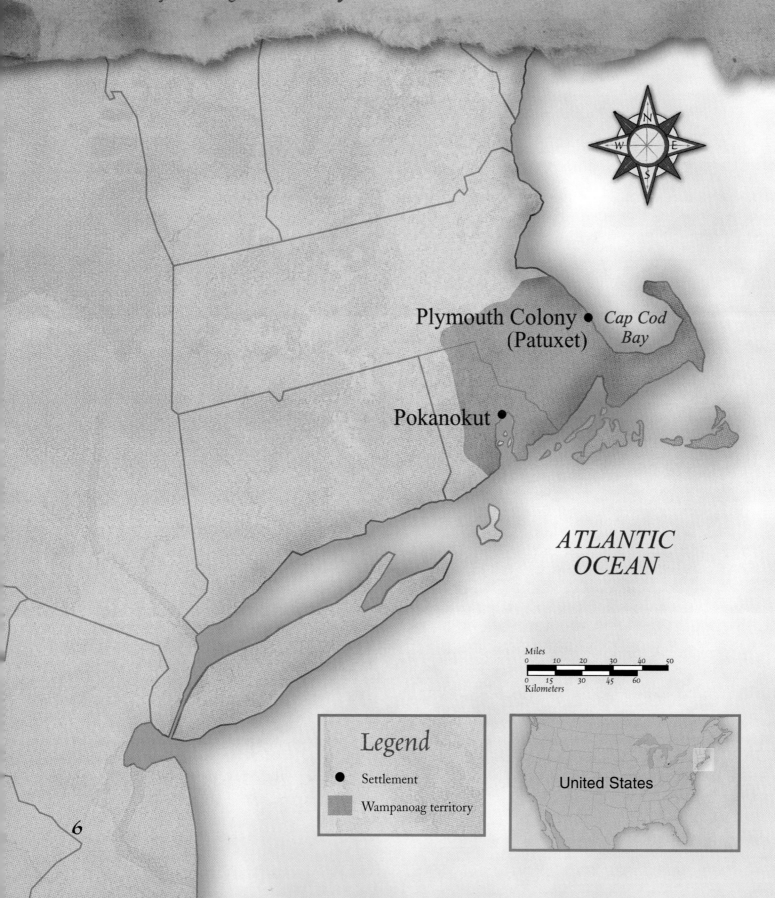

Wampanoag Territory, 1620s

Plymouth Colony ● (Patuxet)

Cap Cod Bay

Pokanokut ●

ATLANTIC OCEAN

Miles
0 10 20 30 40 50

0 15 30 45 60
Kilometers

Legend

● Settlement

▢ Wampanoag territory

United States

Squanto set up a meeting between Massasoit and John Carver, the first governor of Plymouth Colony. Massasoit and Carver met in the colony's meetinghouse. A drum and trumpet blast welcomed the men to peace talks. Carver and Massasoit shared a meal and talked with Squanto's help. The peace talks then began. Squanto repeated what the two men said in their own languages.

With Squanto's help, Massasoit and Carver reached a peace **treaty**. The treaty signed by Massasoit and the settlers at Plymouth lasted for 50 years. Until his death in 1661, Massasoit remained a friend and **ally** of the English.

Squanto stayed with the settlers at Plymouth Colony and helped them through rough times. His work as an **interpreter** helped make one of the most successful treaties between Indians and settlers. In later years, Squanto used his ability to speak English to gain power among the native people and settlers at Plymouth Colony.

The treaty reached by Massasoit and Governor John Carver lasted for 50 years. ➡

CHAPTER 2

Life in a Wampanoag Village

Wampanoag women and children worked together to gather and prepare food. ➡️

The Wampanoag have lived for thousands of years in the areas near present-day Plymouth, Massachusetts. It was in this wooded area along the coast of New England that Squanto was born. Some historians believe he was born in 1585. The exact date and year of Squanto's birth are unknown. No birth records were kept at that time.

Squanto was a member of the Patuxet tribe. The Patuxet were part of the Wampanoag **confederacy**. This group of 60 villages traded together, shared **feast** days, and helped each other in war. Leaders of different tribes often met together.

The Wampanoag made their home in parts of what is today Massachusetts and Rhode Island. Wampanoag means "people of the first light."

In Wampanoag villages, families lived in houses called **wetus**. These one-room houses were made from tall, young trees. One end of the tree was stuck in the ground. The other end of the tree was tied to a pole at the top of the house frame. In summer, these houses were covered with mats made of sturdy cattail leaves. During the winter, the Wampanoag covered their houses with tree bark. When families moved, they took the mats from the *wetus* and left the frames behind.

▲ *Wampanoag families worked together to gather food. The Wampanoag lived in houses called* wetus *as shown in this painting from the late 1800s.*

Wampanoag tribes often returned to the same areas year after year. During the winter months, Wampanoag families would live together in villages. In spring, families would move to their own individual homesites near the coast.

Nothing is known about Squanto's childhood, parents, or family. Historians believe his childhood was similar to that of other Wampanoag children during that time.

Children learned about the land through stories. They listened to grandparents talk about the history, traditions, and laws of their tribe. The Wampanoag people told stories about the land, plants, and animals. Adults taught children to treat all living things with respect.

During the spring and summer, Wampanoag boys helped their mothers weed fields and pick crops.

Children helped scare away birds that tried to eat corn and beans growing in the fields.

Wampanoag boys fished for trout and pike in the clear streams that flowed through the land. They learned how to bait bone hooks with lobster meat. Boys trapped small animals in the woods around the village. Boys learned how to make stone tools such as arrowheads and knives.

Wampanoag children tramped through the thick woods picking raspberries and huckleberries. Children filled baskets full of wild onions, acorns, and chestnuts. Much of the food would be dried and stored for the winter months.

Collecting food was just one of the many ways Wampanoag children helped their villages. As they grew older, boys and girls had different roles in village life.

Corn Bread

The Wampanoag Indians depended on corn as their main source of food. Squanto taught English settlers at Plymouth how to plant corn. The Wampanoag ground dried corn into a flour-like powder. During winter, children kept this powder in pouches to eat as a snack. The Wampanoag also used this powder to make bread. Use the following recipe to make traditional Wampanoag corn bread using modern ingredients.

What You Need

Ingredients

1 8-ounce (240-gram) can of whole kernel corn

1 egg

⅓ cup (80 mL) milk

1 6.5-ounce (195-gram) package corn muffin mix

Equipment

can opener

strainer

mixing bowl

liquid measuring cup

mixing spoon

8-inch by 8-inch (20-centimeter by 20-centimeter) baking pan

nonstick cooking spray

oven mitts

butter knife

What You Do

1. Preheat oven to 350°F (180°C).
2. Open the corn and pour into a strainer to drain. Set corn aside.
3. Add the egg and milk to the muffin mix.
4. Use a mixing spoon to combine ingredients.
5. Stir corn into batter.
6. Coat the baking pan with nonstick cooking spray.
7. Pour batter into baking pan.
8. Bake the bread for 25 to 30 minutes. Bread should be golden brown on top when done.
9. Use oven mitts to remove pan from oven.
10. With a butter knife, cut corn bread into small pieces. Serve warm or cold.
11. Serve corn bread with honey, if desired.

Makes 12 servings

CHAPTER 3

Growing Up Wampanoag

*Wampanoag boys often
practiced their skills with
bows and arrows.* ➡

Wampanoag boys learned
important skills by playing games. They
played games and sports that helped them
grow strong. Boys swam in the lakes near camp.
They became strong and swift by racing against each other.
Boys often practiced shooting bows and arrows.

Wampanoag boys took on more duties as they got older. By the age of 11, many
boys began special training. Wampanoag boys had to prove their strength and skills
as a **warrior**.

Older warriors chose boys for this special training. It was an honor for a Wampanoag boy to be chosen for warrior training. Not all boys were lucky enough to be warriors. Only the strongest and smartest Wampanoag boys were chosen for this training.

Once they were chosen, the boys would leave their families. They would train with older warriors from the village. The boys' fathers or uncles also would guide them through the difficult training.

Young warriors had to complete difficult tasks during training. The boys had to run through thick woods and patches of thorny bushes. As they ran, older adults often would slap them on their shins.

Boys had to drink a liquid made from bitter herbs. The young warriors often got sick after swallowing the liquid. They had to keep drinking the bitter liquid until it no longer made them sick.

Surviving alone in the wilderness was another part of warrior training. Fathers or uncles would lead the young boys into the woods. The boys would be left alone in the woods for weeks or even months. Boys often completed this training during the winter months when food was hard to find.

Wampanoag boys had to use their knowledge of the land to survive. Wampanoag boys would hunt and trap animals. Boys made stone tools. They collected wild foods, like berries, nuts, and vegetables.

If they could survive the bitter cold, it proved that the boys were ready to be adults. When they returned from their training, Wampanoag boys became warriors and adult members of the tribe.

Historians believe Wampanoag warriors met with leaders during councils. They talked with leaders about the needs of their people. These warriors also would advise leaders during war times. Wampanoag leaders would send warriors to meet with other tribes. Warriors were role models for others in the village.

These warriors also set up a special ceremony for their village leader. The warriors would choose a day and time for people to bring baskets of corn to the leader.

The corn would be piled up outside the leader's house. Warriors would thank the people for their gifts. The leader would collect the corn and then give gifts to the people.

These ceremonies and traditions had been a part of the Wampanoag way of life for years. But the Wampanoag people and their way of life changed when European ships landed on the shores of New England.

14

◄

When training to become warriors, Wampanoag boys had to hunt for their own food. They needed to survive in the woods for several weeks.

Ring and Pin Game

The ring and pin game was a popular activity for many North American Indians, including the Wampanoag. A small ring or hoop was attached by a string to a wooden spear. Players would try to catch the ring on the spear. Wampanoag made this game from different materials, including wood, bones, and animal skins.

What You Need

Wooden or plastic hoop about
    3 inches (8 centimeters)
    in diameter
Dowel stick, 12 inches
    (30 centimeters) long
Paint

Paintbrush
Craft beads
Feathers
Scissors
Thick string

What You Do

1. Decorate the hoop and dowel with paint, beads, or feathers.

2. With a scissors, cut a piece of string 24 inches (61 centimeters) long.

3. Tie one end of the string to the top of the dowel stick.

4. Tie the other end of the string to the hoop.

How to Play

1. Hold the dowel stick vertically.

2. Swing the hoop up in the air.

3. Try to catch the hoop with the stick.

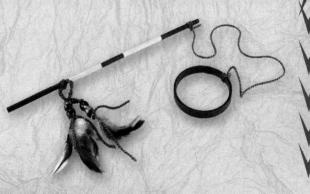

CHAPTER 4
Kidnapped

➤ *The* Mayflower *and other European ships became a common sight along the New England coast in the 1600s.*

The Wampanoag's way of life changed in the early 1600s. Explorers and traders from England and Spain traveled to what is now the New England coast. Many people in England believed the area was rich in gold and other valuable resources. In 1607, English businessmen hired Captain George Weymouth to explore the New England coast. Weymouth and his crew sailed down the coast of what is today Maine until they reached Massachusetts. Weymouth began exploring the thick woodland area. He did not find any gold.

Weymouth and his crew met many native people from tribes in the area, including the Wampanoag. Weymouth thought people in England would want to see the native people. He decided to take some native men to England.

The native men did not want to go with Weymouth. Weymouth took the men by force. The English captain later wrote how he dragged two men by their hair onto the ship. He used food to trick three other Indian men onto the ship.

Today, historians disagree on whether Squanto was among the men **kidnapped** by Weymouth's crew.

In the early 1600s, some explorers took native people against their will to be sold as slaves in England and Spain. ➡

Some historians believe Squanto was one of these men. Other historians believe Squanto did not have his first contact with the English until 1614.

In 1614, an English ship reached the shores of New England. John Smith was captain of the ship. Smith's crew was sent to map the area.

When the mapping trip was over, Smith returned to England on another ship. Smith put Englishman Thomas Hunt in charge of his crew. Hunt was a mean and greedy man. He knew people in Spain would pay a great deal of money for slaves.

Hunt invited 27 native men onto his ship. Historians agree that Squanto was one of the native men on Hunt's ship. The Indians believed they were going to trade beaver skins. Squanto was to be an interpreter. But Hunt's invitation was a trap. He took the native men against their will.

Hunt took the men to Spain, where he tried to sell them as slaves. Local priests learned of Hunt's plan. They rescued Squanto and some of the other native men. Squanto lived with the priests until 1618.

Squanto then made his way to England. Historians agree that Squanto lived with Sir Fernando Gorges in England. Gorges owned much of what is today Maine. Gorges taught Squanto some English. Squanto soon learned to speak English very well. Gorges began using him as a guide and interpreter.

Gorges wanted to explore more of the New England area and begin trading with native tribes. But many tribes were angry with the English after Hunt took their men. Violence had broken out between some native tribes and traders.

In 1619, Gorges sent explorer Thomas Dermer and Squanto to New England. Squanto was to help Dermer trade with the Indians.

Dermer and Squanto returned to Patuxet. The men found that the entire village was deserted. Squanto and Dermer set out to find the Patuxet. During the trip, Dermer was injured during an attack by an enemy tribe. He later died from his injuries.

After the attack, Squanto went to live with Massasoit at Pokanoket. Massasoit told Squanto that a disease had killed all of the Patuxet people. From 1616 to 1619, an unknown disease spread through the Wampanoag and other tribes in Massachusetts. Historians believe that European fishermen and explorers spread the disease to Indians in the area. Most tribes lost countless men, women, and children to the deadly disease.

The Wampanoag lost more people to the disease than other tribes. Many Wampanoag warriors died. Massasoit feared the loss left his people open to attacks from enemy tribes. He knew Squanto could speak with the settlers. Massasoit believed Squanto's ability to speak English could help protect the Wampanoag. Massasoit would soon learn the value of Squanto and his skill of speaking English.

CHAPTER 5

A Treaty for Peace

English settlers built Plymouth Colony at the former site of Squanto's village of Patuxet. ➤

In November 1620, English settlers aboard the *Mayflower* arrived on the shores of what is now Massachusetts. The Wampanoag and settlers did not meet right away. Instead, the Wampanoag watched the settlers as they explored area lakes and woods.

In late December, the English began building a settlement on an area of high ground. Trees, stumps, and rocks had already been cleared from the land. They called it Plymouth Colony. The English had chosen to live at the former site of Squanto's village, Patuxet.

Massasoit watched as the English struggled to build homes and make a life on unfamiliar land. The Wampanoag leader decided it was time to begin talks with the English. Massasoit sent Samoset to meet with the English.

On March 16, 1621, Samoset quietly walked into the Plymouth settlement. He surprised the settlers when he welcomed them in English. Samoset had learned some of the language by trading with fishermen.

Samoset told the English about the Patuxet village. He explained how the Patuxet had cleared the land and worked the fields that now stood empty.

Samoset told Massasoit that the settlers wanted to make peace. The Wampanoag leader knew the English also had lost many settlers to disease. Only 50 settlers were left at Plymouth Colony. The settlers needed food and supplies to survive.

Massasoit believed the English and their weapons would be helpful to the Wampanoag. In return, his people could help the English if they were attacked. Massasoit decided to visit Plymouth Colony.

On March 22, 1621, Squanto, Samoset, and three others met with settlers at Plymouth Colony. Squanto told the settlers that Massasoit wanted to hold peace talks with the English. The settlers agreed to the meeting.

▲ *Governor John Carver greeted Massasoit as he entered Plymouth Colony.*
This painting of their meeting was done in the late 1800s.

Plymouth settler William Bradford wrote that the leaders greeted each other and kissed each other's hands. They then sat down on pillows. Squanto sat with them. Squanto **translated** for the two men. Soon, the men agreed on a treaty.

In the treaty, Massasoit said his people would not harm or steal from the settlers. Carver and Massasoit agreed to help each other during war. They promised not to carry weapons when visiting each other. Massasoit agreed to tell other tribes about the treaty. If willing, these tribes would have to follow the treaty. The two sides agreed that King James II was part of the treaty. Massasoit and the English king were now allies.

After the meeting, Massasoit and Samoset returned to their villages. Squanto realized the English had much to learn about their new home. He decided to stay at Plymouth.

The Treaty of 1621

The Treaty of 1621 marked a time of peace for the English settlers and Wampanoag. Plymouth Colony Governor John Carver and Wampanoag leader Massasoit led the peace talks. No record exists of the treaty talks translated by Squanto. The original treaty does not exist. The treaty was recorded in journals kept by some settlers at Plymouth Colony.

The Treaty of 1621 lasted for 50 years. The agreement began to fall apart as more English settlers arrived. New settlements were built on native people's lands. The settlers and native people disagreed about who controlled the land.

The relationship between settlers and native peoples grew worse after the deaths of William Bradford in 1657 and Massasoit in 1661. Massasoit's son Wamsutta took over as leader. Wamsutta became ill shortly after visiting Plymouth Colony and died in 1662. Many Wampanoag blamed the English for his death.

Another of Massasoit's sons, Metacom, became leader after his brother's death. The English often called him King Philip. In 1671, Metacom was forced to sign a new treaty that put the English government in charge of his people. The Treaty of 1621 was over.

In 1675, war began between settlers and native people over land rights. The battles became known as King Philip's War. Metacom was killed in 1676. The war ended soon after his death.

◀

Plymouth Colony leaders greeted Massasoit at the start of peace talks. The Wampanoag did not wear large headdresses as shown in this painting from the 1800s. No painting was done at the time of the treaty talks.

CHAPTER 6
Power Plays

Squanto and the English faced many challenges at Plymouth. Squanto soon was busy serving as an interpreter, guide, and teacher for the settlers. The English needed his help. They had struggled through their first winter in the strange land. Many settlers were sick. Others were weak from a lack of food. The settlers' houses barely kept out the wind and rain.

Squanto became an important part of life at Plymouth. He taught the settlers when to plant crops. The best time to plant seeds, Squanto said, was when oak buds grew to the size of a mouse's ear.

He showed the settlers how to plant corn by setting four kernels in a mound of dirt along with two or three fish. The Wampanoag did not always bury fish when they planted seeds. The land in the Plymouth area had been farmed for many years. The soil was poor. Fish were needed to **fertilize** the soil.

Squanto taught the English about the Wampanoag way of life. He showed them how to live off the land. Squanto taught them how to hoe fields with clamshells.

↟ *Squanto showed settlers how to use fish when planting to help fertilize the soil. This drawing shows how artist Charles W. Jeffreys (1869–1951) pictured Squanto and the settlers.*

He showed them which plants were safe to eat. Squanto showed them plants that could be used for medicine.

Squanto took the settlers to riverbanks. He taught them to catch fish in the rivers and streams. He showed them how to catch eels by tramping on the mud until long, fat eels popped out.

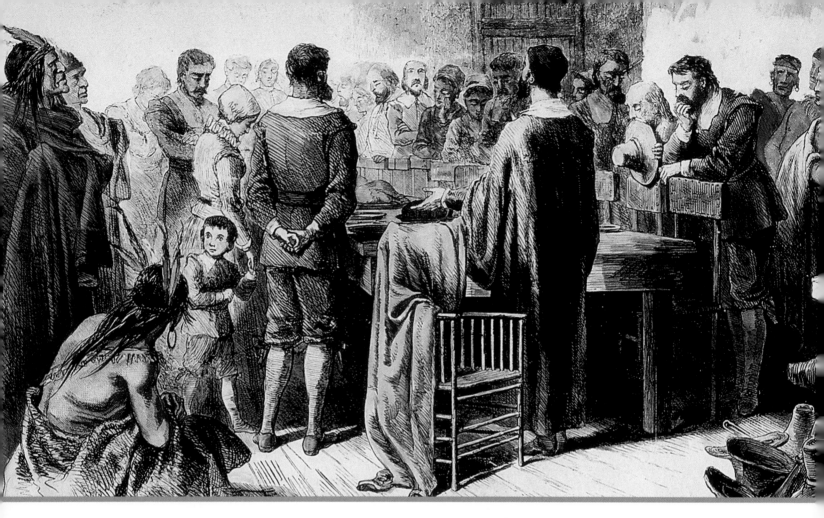

▲ *In 1622, Wampanoag and people at Plymouth Colony joined in a harvest celebration that is now called the first Thanksgiving. This 1870 painting of the event is not a historically accurate picture. About 90 Wampanoag men attended the celebration with about 50 people from Plymouth.*

The English learned many things from Squanto. After the harvest, the settlers had enough food for the entire village. They also had plenty of food to dry and save for the winter months. Bradford, who was now governor of Plymouth, remembered when his people were starving. Now, the 50 settlers at Plymouth Colony had plenty of food. Bradford decided to hold a harvest celebration.

Massasoit and 90 of his people joined in the feast. Massasoit and his people brought deer and other food to Plymouth. The harvest celebration lasted three days.

No historical record mentions Squanto attending the celebration, now called the first Thanksgiving. Historians believe he was at the celebration because he was living in Plymouth during that time.

After the celebration, Squanto continued to live with the English. Early in 1622, the Narragansett sent the English a bundle of arrows tied in rattlesnake skin. Squanto told Governor Bradford the skin and arrows were meant as a threat.

Bradford wanted the Narragansett to know the English were not afraid. Bradford took out the arrows. He stuffed the skin with gunpowder and bullets. He sent the skin back to the Narragansett chief. The Narragansett learned not to threaten the English again.

Squanto gained power in the Wampanoag community. His many travels and ability to speak English earned him a place of honor and power. But Squanto wanted more.

Squanto tried to become a more powerful leader by telling lies to the Wampanoag. He told his people that the English had buried a deadly disease at the colony. The English had only buried barrels of gunpowder.

Squanto knew his people would take the threat of disease seriously. The Wampanoag would be afraid and turn to Squanto for help. Squanto hinted that he could control whether the English released the disease. The Wampanoag people believed Squanto. He became more powerful.

In March 1622, the English wrote that Squanto caused more trouble. Squanto told the English that the Narragansett and Massasoit planned to attack Plymouth. Squanto wanted both groups to think that he could control war and peace between them. The English did not believe Squanto.

"Thus by degrees we began to discover Tisquantum (Squanto), whose ends were only to make himself great in the eyes of [his] country-men, by means of his nearness and favor with us, not caring who fell so he stood."
—Edward Winslow, Secretary of Plymouth Colony, 1624

Massasoit was angered when he heard about Squanto's lies. He told the settlers that the Wampanoag wanted peace. He asked the English to turn over Squanto.

Bradford refused. More settlers would soon arrive. Both the settlers and Wampanoag would need Squanto's skills as an interpreter. Massasoit never again asked to take Squanto prisoner.

Despite Squanto's lies, he and Bradford continued to go on trading trips together. In late 1622, Bradford and Squanto sailed south from Plymouth toward Cape Cod.

While on the ship, Squanto became sick. He began to bleed from his nose. Within a few days, Squanto was dead.

The English felt Squanto's death was a great loss. They had lost their adviser and interpreter.

Squanto remains a popular figure in many history books. He is known as a brave man who survived the pain of kidnapping and helped the settlers in Plymouth.

Today, many Wampanoag remember Squanto much differently. Many Wampanoag do not agree with Squanto's popular role as a friend of the English. They believe he became more interested in personal power than in helping his own people.

Chronology

1585?
Squanto is born; historians do not know the exact date or place of his birth.

1616 to 1619
A deadly disease hits the eastern coast; the disease spreads to the Wampanoag and kills entire villages of people.

1619
Squanto returns to Patuxet to find his village deserted.

March 1621
With Squanto translating, Massasoit makes a peace treaty with the English.

Late 1614
Thomas Hunt kidnaps Squanto and 26 other Wampanoag men; he tries to sell the men as slaves in Spain.

1620
The English build Plymouth Colony on the site of Squanto's former village of Patuxet.

1622
Squanto dies on board an English ship during a trading trip.

Late 1621
Massasoit and 90 Wampanoag join Squanto and settlers at Plymouth for a harvest celebration.

Glossary

ally (AL-eye)—a person or country that gives support to another person or country

breechclout (BREECH-klout)—a short, skirtlike garment that is tied around the waist and has open slits on the sides

confederacy (kuhn-FED-ur-uh-see)—a union of towns or tribes with a common goal

feast (FEEST)—a large meal attended by many people on a special occasion

fertilize (FUR-tuh-lize)—to put a rich substance on land to improve the soil and make crops grow; the Wampanoag used fish to fertilize their cornfields.

interpreter (in-TUR-prit-ter)—someone who can tell others what is said in another language

kidnap (KID-nap)—to capture someone and keep that person as a prisoner

translate (transs-LATE)—to change words from one language to another

treaty (TREE-tee)—an official agreement between two or more groups or countries

warrior (WOR-ee-ur)—a person who fights in battle

wetu (WEE-too)—a round building with a curved roof that is covered with grass, leaves, or animal skins

Read More

Bial, Raymond. *The Wampanoag*. Lifeways. New York: Benchmark Books, 2003.

Dell, Pamela. *The Plymouth Colony*. Let Freedom Ring. Mankato, Minn.: Bridgestone Books, 2004.

Riehecky, Janet. *The Wampanoag: The People of the First Light*. American Indian Nations. Mankato, Minn.: Bridgestone Books, 2003.

Waters, Kate. *Giving Thanks: The 1621 Harvest Feast*. New York: Scholastic, 2001.

Internet Sites

FactHound offers a safe, fun way to find Internet sites related to this book. All of the sites on FactHound have been researched by our staff.

Here's how:

1. Visit *www.facthound.com*
2. Type in this special code **0736824464** for age-appropriate sites. Or enter a search word related to this book for a more general search.
3. Click on the **Fetch It** button.

FactHound will fetch the best sites for you!

Useful Addresses

The Children's Museum
300 Congress Street
Boston, MA 02210-1034

Mashpee Wampanoag Indian Museum
Route 130
Mashpee, MA 02649

Plimoth Plantation
P.O. Box 1620
Plymouth, MA 02362

Wampanoag Tribe of Gay Head (Aquinnah)
20 Black Brook Road
Aquinnah, MA 02535–1546

Index